The Science of Cars

By Larry Heiman

Illustrated by the Disney Storybook Artists

Special thanks to Leslie Mark Kendall, Chief Curator at
Petersen Automotive Museum, Los Angeles, California

Lerner Publications ◆ Minneapolis

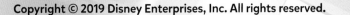

Lerner Publications Company
A division of Lerner Publishing Group, Inc.
241 First Avenue North
Minneapolis, MN 55401 USA

For reading levels and more information, look up this title at www.lernerbooks.com.

Main body text set in Mikado.
Typeface provided by HVD Fonts.

Library of Congress Cataloging-in-Publication Data

The Cataloging-in-Publication Data for *The Science of Cars: A Cars Discovery Book*
   is on file at the Library of Congress.
ISBN 978-1-5415-3261-8 (lib. bdg.)
ISBN 978-1-5415-3280-9 (pbk.)
ISBN 978-1-5415-3265-6 (eb pdf)

33614081427816

Manufactured in the United States of America
1-44851-35721-3/1/2018

CONTENTS

WHAT IS A CAR?

Lightning McQueen's friends come in many different shapes and sizes. They are all marvelous machines that use their own power to get from one place to another—or quickly around a racetrack. Let's take a peek under the hood and explore the amazing machines we call cars.

It's a Big Group!

Cars are part of the big group of vehicles called automobiles, or **motorized vehicles**. In that group, you will find cars, trucks, buses, and vans. You will even find tractors, bulldozers, and fire trucks. There are different kinds of vehicles for different kinds of jobs.

What Every Vehicle Needs

Every vehicle has an **engine**. The engine uses some kind of **fuel** for energy. A gasoline engine converts gasoline, or gas, into motion to get a car moving. An engine in an electric vehicle is called a **motor**. An electric car delivers power from the batteries to the motor.

Let's Get Rolling!

Fuel runs the engine or motor, which sends power to the wheels. That power makes the wheels move. Let's find out more about how these great machines work.

CARS TO RACE AND RIDE

Sterling owns the Rust-eze Racing Center. Cars train there to become better racers. But what exactly makes a car a **race car**? What does a race car have that a family car or commuter car doesn't?

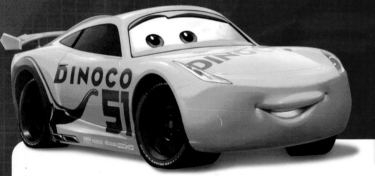

Fast Cars

A race car like Cruz Ramirez is built for speed! Her **body**, engine, and tires help her go as fast as she safely can on the racetrack.

Family Cars

A family car or a minivan is not for racing. Its job is to carry you and your friends or family on the road—not on the racetrack. It is built to keep you safe and comfortable.

Commuter Cars

Any car, except a race car, can be a commuter car. Its main job is to travel from home to work and back every day. Many of the best commuter cars are small, comfortable, and safe.

ALL SYSTEMS GO!

Smokey was the Fabulous Hudson Hornet's crew chief. If a car is in trouble, he can find the trouble and fix it! Smokey understands that a car is made up of many different systems. All the systems have to work together to keep a car running.

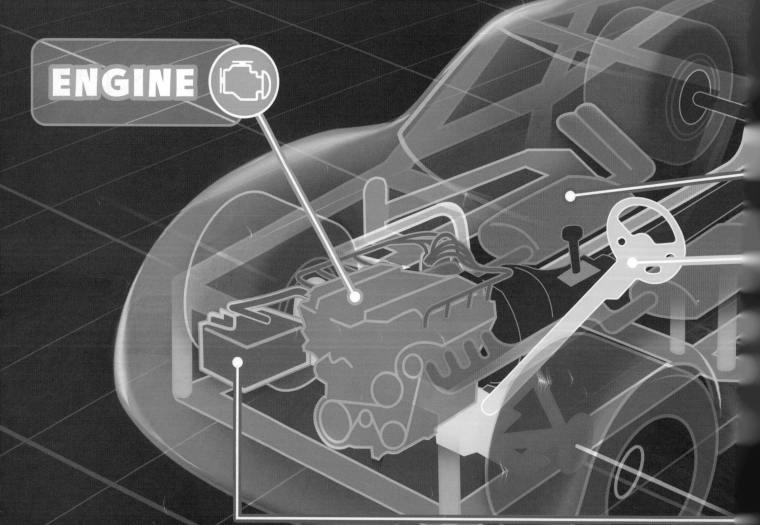

ENGINE

FUEL SYSTEM

DRIVETRAIN

TIRES & BRAKES

EXHAUST

STEERING

BODY & CHASSIS

ELECTRICAL SYSTEM

MAKING THE METAL MOVE

Doc was Lightning's crew chief. Doc knew that every car starts with several main systems—the engine, the **drivetrain**, the **chassis**, the steering, and the brakes.

The Engine

A car without an engine will not move. The engine is the thing that all the other systems count on. The engine provides the power to all the systems in the car.

The Drivetrain

The engine's main job is to burn fuel and turn it into energy. That energy is **transferred** to the drivetrain, which is connected to the back or sometimes the side of the engine. The drivetrain delivers the power produced in the engine to the wheels so the car can move. The **gears** in the **transmission** help control how fast or slow the car goes.

Transmission

The Body and the Chassis

A chassis is the supporting frame of the car. A car's engine, tires, and other mechanical parts are bolted to the chassis.

The body of a car is made up of large panels. The body is designed to protect a car's riders. A car's engine, transmission, and other systems can sometimes be found within the body.

Chassis with wheels and tires

Unibody design with wheels and tires

In many race cars, trucks, and older cars like Doc or Smokey, the chassis and the body are made as two separate pieces and then fastened together. But most cars made today have a **unibody** design. The frame and the basic body shell are made together. A chassis and body that is one big piece is easier and faster to build. A car with a unibody design is also lighter, quieter, and safer.

FUEL THE MACHINE

Before leaving the Cotter Pin, River Scott stops to fill up at the gasoline pump outside the door. Why? Because gas keeps a car's engine running! Gas is the fuel still used by most cars today—but that is changing.

Explosive Power

Cutaway of an internal combustion engine

An engine that uses gas has a special name. It is called an **internal combustion** engine. *Internal* means "inside." **Combustion** means "burning." Fuel is pumped into the engine where—at just the right time—a tiny electrical spark sets off an explosion. The force of that explosion is the power that makes the wheels move.

fuel tank

fuel pump

fuel line

engine

Reducing Pollution

The fuel internal combustion engines burn is not good for our air. More and more cars are being manufactured without internal combustion engines. Their engines use electricity for fuel, not gas. Instead of stopping to fill the car's gas tank, a driver stops to recharge the car's big batteries.

Get Comfortable

Electricity can help a car run. You can also thank electricity for a lot of things that keep you comfortable inside a car. The radio, lights, heater, windows, and sometimes even the seats all use electricity.

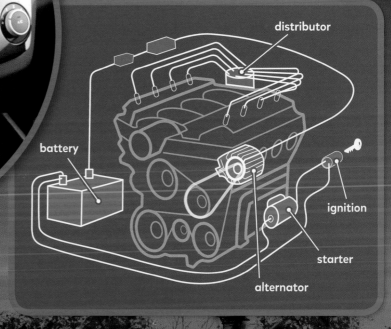

distributor

battery

ignition

starter

alternator

THROTTLE UP!

Cruz Ramirez is a fast racer. She knows that the engine is the power center of a car. Most engines use gasoline for fuel, but they also need electricity. **Spark plugs** deliver the electricity needed to **ignite** the fuel inside the engine. This creates the energy needed to make the car move.

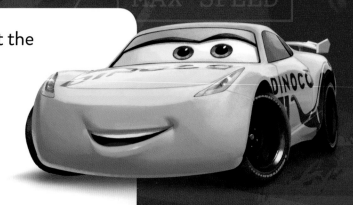

Inside a Gas Engine

Inside a car's engine, there are one or two rows of closed, sealed tubes called **cylinders**. Tiny explosions inside the cylinders make energy that becomes the force that moves the car. There are thousands of these explosions every minute! Most passenger cars have four cylinders. But bigger cars, trucks, and race cars could have six, eight, ten, and even twelve cylinders. The more cylinders an engine has, the more power the engine can usually make.

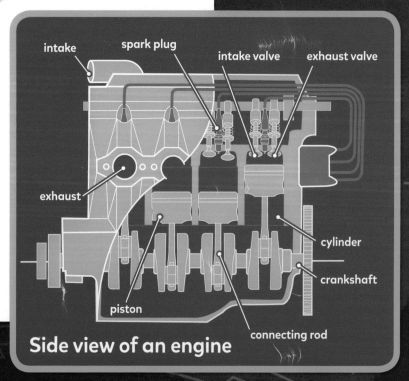

intake   spark plug   intake valve   exhaust valve

exhaust

cylinder

crankshaft

piston

connecting rod

Side view of an engine

It's Explosive

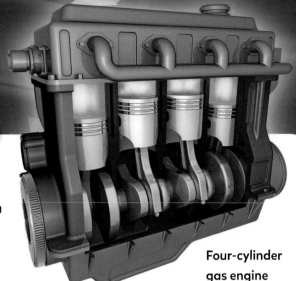

Let's take a look inside a four-cylinder engine and see where and how these explosions happen. Each cylinder goes through four steps, called **strokes**.

Four-cylinder gas engine

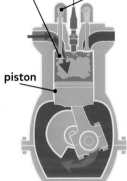

intake valve   camshaft

piston

Front view of cylinder

Stroke 1: Intake

During the **intake** stroke, the **piston** moves down from the top of the cylinder. The **camshaft** opens the **intake valve**. A few drops of gas enter the cylinder, and the intake valve closes tight.

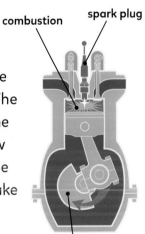

combustion   spark plug

crankshaft

Stroke 3: Combustion

The **distributor** sends electricity through a wire to the spark plug. The tiny spark makes the air and gas mixture ignite and **expand**. This explosion pushes the piston back down. That force turns the **crankshaft** to make the wheels move.

compression

Stroke 2: Compression

The piston is pushed back up and squeezes the air and gas tightly together. This **compression** makes the explosion more powerful.

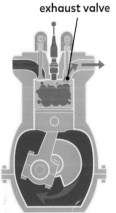

exhaust valve

Stroke 4: Exhaust

During the **exhaust** stroke, the piston moves back up and the camshaft opens the **exhaust valve**. The piston pushes the burned fuel out of the cylinder through the open exhaust valve and into the car's **exhaust system**.

One cylinder by itself would not have the power to move a modern car. But most car engines have at least four cylinders working together at the same time—and they make a superpowerful team!

GET INTO GEAR

The crankshaft in a car's engine rotates thousands of times every minute! It is connected to the transmission, which controls the amount of power going from the engine to the wheels. The transmission keeps the engine from working too hard. It also makes sure that the wheels get the power they need for the speed the driver wants. Experienced racers like Jackson Storm and Lightning McQueen know the art of choosing the right gear at the right time to stay in the race.

Lots of Gears!

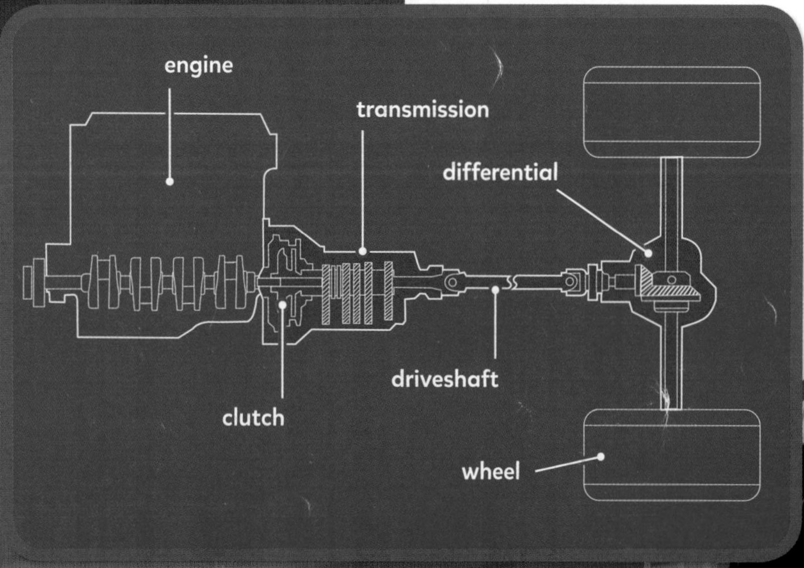

The transmission attaches to the engine. There are lots of gears in the transmission. The gears work together to transfer the engine's power to the wheels.

engine

transmission

differential

clutch

driveshaft

wheel

Manual Transmission

There are two main kinds of car transmissions. One is **manual transmission**, and the other is **automatic transmission**.

With a manual transmission, the driver decides when to shift the gears for the best power. It takes skill and practice. The driver takes one foot off the gas and steps on the **clutch pedal** with the other foot. This **disconnects** the engine from the transmission. The driver then moves the gear selector into gear, takes his or her foot off the clutch pedal, and steps on the gas again.

Gear selector for manual transmission

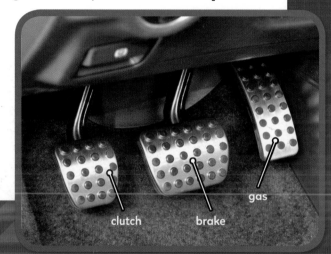

clutch   brake   gas

Automatic Transmission

Cars with automatic transmissions do all the shifting themselves. To get the car into gear, the driver moves the gearshift to either D for drive or R for reverse. The transmission does the rest! The transmission uses the best gear for the engine, while the driver concentrates on the road. There is no clutch pedal in a car with automatic transmission. The driver has a gas pedal and a brake pedal.

Gearshift for automatic transmission

PUSH ME, PULL ME

Racing legend Louise "Barnstormer" Nash has a **rear-wheel drive (RWD)** system. But what exactly does that mean? What is the difference between rear-wheel drive, **front-wheel drive (FWD)**, **four-wheel drive (4WD)**, and **all-wheel drive (AWD)**? It's good to know what kind of **drive system** a car has, because that tells which wheels actually get the power to make the car move.

Rear-wheel drive system

Rear-Wheel Drive

Most older cars, trucks, buses, and some sports cars on the road today have a rear-wheel drive system. This means that the power moves from the engine through the transmission to the rear or back wheels of the car. The rear wheels push the car forward. Most race car drivers prefer rear-wheel drive. They believe it helps the car perform better when swinging through tight curves on the track. The car has better balance with the heavy engine in front and the push from the back.

Front-Wheel Drive

Front-wheel drive system

Many passenger cars built today have front-wheel drive, where the engine's power is delivered to the front wheels. With power coming from the front wheels, the car is pulled instead of pushed. Drivers of family cars and commuter cars feel they are easier to drive. With the heavy engine adding to the weight in front, many drivers feel this system gives better **traction** on hills and in snow. Front-wheel drive is also safer for turning.

Using All the Wheels

An all-wheel drive system can change which **axle** has the power. If the car senses the wheels on one axle are slipping, it will send power to the other axle to get better traction. This can help keep a car moving over mud, wet roads, snow, ice, or sand. All-wheel drive systems are found in many newer family vehicles and SUVs.

All-wheel and four-wheel drive systems

A four-wheel drive vehicle delivers the engine's power to all four wheels at the same time. Having this control can be great for driving where there are no roads at all—like up a steep dirt hill, over rocks, or through a stream! Each of the wheels gets power for maximum traction.

HIT THE BRAKES

Ka-chow! Lightning knows how to zip around superfast on a racetrack. But he also knows that being able to *stop* is just as important as being able to *go*. It's all about the brakes!

Drum Brakes

Legends like River Scott and Junior Moon have **drum brakes**. Racers like Lightning McQueen, Jackson Storm, and most modern vehicles on the road today use **disc brakes**. Both brake systems will stop a car, but disc brakes do it better.

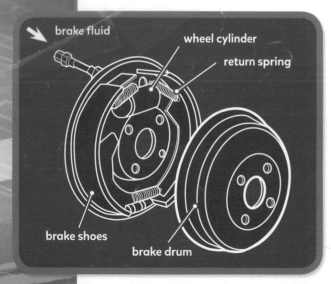

brake fluid
wheel cylinder
return spring
brake shoes
brake drum

The drum in a drum brake system is made out of heavy steel. When a driver with drum brakes steps on the brake pedal, it pushes two curved **brake shoes** against the inside of the spinning drum. This causes heat and **friction**. The friction slows down the wheel. You can't see the brake shoes in a drum brake system because they are covered by the drum.

Disc Brakes

Disc brakes have a clamp called a **caliper**. **Brake pads** inside the caliper squeeze both sides of the disc at the same time. This slows down the wheels and the car. The disc can be made out of iron, but many—especially those on race cars—are made from lighter carbon **composite** material or **ceramic**.

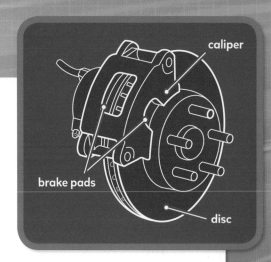

Most drivers like disc brakes better than drum brakes. Disc brakes are stronger and last a long time. They cool down faster because they are open to the air. Drum brakes are covered up and can't cool down as fast. They can get too hot to work and usually wear out sooner.

Extra Help for Slippery Roads

Good racers know many tricks to keep from losing control of their cars. Most cars made today have an extra helper with their brakes—the **antilock braking system**, or ABS.

Sensors on every wheel measure its speed. Special pumps and a computer can tell when a tire starts to skid on a wet road. When that happens, the ABS takes control of the brakes on all four wheels. It does everything it can to keep those wheels from skidding. It works to get the car going straight again. ABS is like having an experienced race car driver take over until the danger is past!

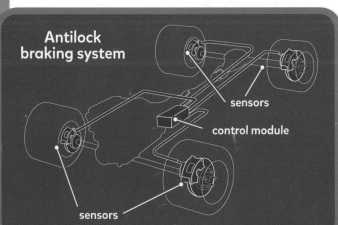

KEEP THE RUBBER ON THE ROAD

There are different tires for different track surfaces. Whether the track is wet or dry, made of asphalt or dirt, Luigi and Guido know the right tire can make the winning difference!

Tires for a Dry Track

Racers are happiest when the track is dry and the weather is mild. On dry days, race cars use special tires called slicks. They got that name because they have no **treads**. They are completely slick!

Slicks Need to Stick!

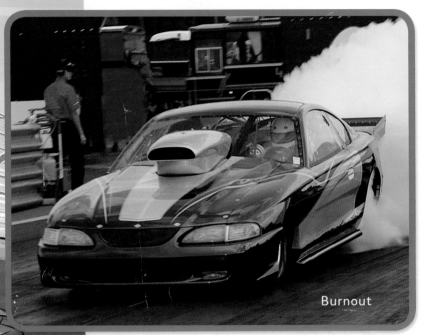

Burnout

Many racers on today's racetracks might take warm-up laps before the flag drops. They will slowly swerve back and forth. They are not practicing steering. They are "scrubbing" their front tires to get them warm and soft so that they will stick to the asphalt on fast turns.

In a **drag race**, where there are no turns, cars need their *back* tires to stick. Drag racers might force only the back tires to spin superfast to make them hot. This is called a **burnout**. Hot tires stick better to the track.

Watch the Weather!

The race officials keep a careful eye on the weather during a long race. If it looks like rain, it may be time for a tire change. Those slicks will not work at all on a wet track. It's time to make a quick **pit stop** and change to "wets." The tread on these tires will help throw the water to the side to keep the car sticking to the track on those slippery laps.

Racing tires don't last very long. A good tire on a passenger car can be safe for thousands of miles of driving. But race car tires, often driving at over 150 miles (241 km) per hour, may need to be changed several times during a single race.

SAFETY FIRST

Sheriff enforces traffic and driving laws to make sure the roads are safe for everyone. Good drivers think about safety all the time. Let's look at some of the things that make cars safe.

Beep-Beep!

One of the first safety features added to cars was the horn. Making a loud noise is a good way to get other drivers to pay attention and stay alert. However, the loud blast from a horn can be shocking. A driver should never use it without a good reason.

Belts and Bags

When a car is racing forward and suddenly crashes into something, it stops. But everything *inside* the car keeps going. Books, cups, and sandwiches go flying through the air. So can the driver and passengers. That's why all modern cars have seat belts and **airbags**. Seat belts hold passengers safely in their seats. Everyone in the car should wear them. An airbag provides extra protection in a crash. In less than a second, a big pillow pops out from inside the car and quickly fills up with air to cushion the driver and any passengers.

An airbag deploying from the steering wheel during a crash test

The Crumple Zone

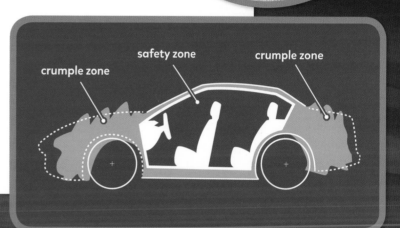

The car is crunched, but you are not! Most modern cars have **crumple zones** in the front and back. Crumple zones soften a crash to protect passengers. The crumple zones are designed to absorb energy in a crash. This keeps the full force of the crash away from the driver and any passengers.

There might be a terrible accident at the racetrack. A car rolls and turns and hits a wall. Parts are flying in all directions. But when the dust clears, the driver stands up and waves to the crowd! The car has completely fallen apart. But it was made to break away from the driver, who was protected in the safety zone.

crumple zone   safety zone   crumple zone

Crash test dummy

Safety Testing

Carmakers constantly come up with new ideas to keep people safe in a crash. Those ideas and designs are tested using life-size models of people. These models are **crash test dummies**. They are built to look and move like humans. Crash test dummies have special sensors that send important information to the carmakers about what happens in a crash. That information tells the designers what needs to change to make the car safer for people in an accident.

NO DRAG, PLEASE!

Next-gen racers like Jackson Storm think a lot about speed and **efficiency**. They will do everything they can to reduce **drag**. *Drag* is exactly what it sounds like—"something that slows you down." The biggest cause of drag is air. Race car manufacturers have a few tricks to make cars more **aerodynamic**. They want air to work with the car instead of slowing it down.

Wings

A wing on a sports car

Air is always rushing over, under, and around a moving car. This creates drag and makes the car work harder to move forward. At the super-high speeds on a racetrack, that air can actually lift the back wheels off the ground. A **wing**, or airfoil, looks like a small, upside-down airplane wing. It is mounted across the back of a race car. The wing pushes the air *up* and forces the back end of the car *down*. This is called **downforce**. Downforce pushes the rear tires of a **Formula One race car** onto the track. The car can speed through a turn faster without spinning out of control.

Spoilers

Piston Cup race cars like Cal Weathers have the same trouble with air as Formula One race cars. But instead of wings, they use **spoilers** to force the airflow around and *away* from the car. The spoiler attaches to the back of the car and forces the air to stream over the top of the car. Without the spoiler, the air could lift the tail end of the car. A rear spoiler reduces drag and helps keep those back tires sticking to the road.

There is such a thing as too much downforce, though. Too much downforce creates drag. So racers always experiment with the angle of their spoilers and wings. They try to find just the right balance between downforce and drag.

A spoiler on a sports car

A sports car with a carbon fiber finish panel

Weight

How much a car weighs can have a big effect on drag, speed, handling, and fuel efficiency. The material that cars are made of has changed over the years. Car frames and bodies used to be made mostly of steel. Steel is strong, but it is also very heavy. Weight creates drag. Drag reduces speed and makes the engine burn more fuel.

Race car designers thought cars could get faster by losing some weight. They began mixing **aluminum** into vehicle bodies. Aluminum is strong like steel but is much lighter.

Some steel and aluminum parts in commuter and race cars are now being replaced with an even lighter material called **carbon fiber**. Carbon fiber is a kind of cloth that can be woven together and piled into layers. Then it is covered with special hard glue called **epoxy**. Car parts made with carbon fiber are stronger than steel and much lighter. A car made with carbon fiber has less weight to push around the track.

GET IN LINE

New cars are built on an **assembly line** at a factory. Lizzie knows all about the assembly line. She is a Ford Model T. The Model T was the first car to be produced on an assembly line. On an assembly line, engines are put together and bodies are formed. Electric wires are connected, and drivetrains are attached. Doors are put in place. Windshields, seats, wheels, and brakes are installed. The modern automobile factory does everything that goes into making a car.

One Step at a Time

Almost every car in the world today came from a factory assembly line. It is called a line because the cars move down in a line to the workers. The workers usually stay in one place. When a car reaches a worker, the worker does the same job on each car.

Cars move down the assembly line to the workers.

Robots Work Hard!

Robots do a lot of work at factories. They are fast and strong. They can do some of the hardest and most dangerous jobs. Robots often build the chassis and car bodies. You will also find robots doing most of the painting. They work in spots that humans cannot reach.

Robots on the assembly line

Paints for Color and Protection

Ramone is an artist. He knows more than any other car about paint and decoration. Some factories use five different kinds of paint to protect a car. One special coat of paint keeps rust away. Another layer of paint protects the car from the sun. The bottom of the car gets painted with an **undercoating**. This keeps dirt from sticking to the bottom of the car. The undercoating also blocks any water from getting between the frame and the body. The busy team of robots in the painting rooms can spend hours finishing just one car. At the end of a day, humans and robots sharing the work on an assembly line can finish hundreds of cars.

Robots on the painting line

Cars at the end of the assembly line are ready for inspection.

29

AMAZING CAR CULTURES

Ramone likes to cruise low 'n' slow, sporting his latest paint job. All around the world, many car owners belong to different car cultures. They have a lot of fun making their cars look different and special. They like to get together and show off their hard work.

Lowriders

Have you ever seen a car hopping up and down while slowly driving down the street? Then you have probably seen a lowrider like Ramone. The bodies of these cars are very, very low to the ground, but they have special **shock absorbers** that can push and pump the wheels up and down whenever the driver wants.

Tuners

Tuners like Wingo are all about freedom of expression. A car is "tuned" by changing, or modifying, its engine, body, or other system to make it go faster.

Hot Rods

A hot rod usually starts as a regular, older American car, like Junior Moon. It gets a new, powerful engine and heavy-duty drivetrain. Its body may be changed a bit too.

START YOUR ENGINES!

Next-gen racers like Bubba Wheelhouse are built for speed. Race cars today are a blend of technology and smart design. Let's take a look at different kinds of race cars, the tracks they run on, and the races they compete in.

Two Kinds of Race Cars

Race cars can be divided into two main types. There are **open-wheel cars** and **closed-wheel cars**. It is easy to tell the difference. A closed-wheel car is one where the wheels are covered by the car's body or fender. **Stock cars** and cars that race on **rally circuits** feature a closed-wheel design. The wheels on an open-wheel car are seen outside the car's main body. Formula One and **Indy cars** are good examples.

An open-wheel Indy car

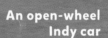

A closed-wheel rally car

Stock Cars

Stock car racing got its name because at first the cars were regular assembly-line, or stock, vehicles.

Then people began making their own changes to these cars. The cars got faster and more powerful, and the races became too dangerous. An organization called **NASCAR** set up rules about the kinds of improvements a car can have. Today, NASCAR races are the most popular races in North America.

The Daytona 500

Stock cars racing at the Daytona 500

NASCAR races feature stock cars, like Bobby Swift. The most famous stock car race is the **Daytona 500** in Daytona Beach, Florida. The Daytona 500 is 500 miles (805 km) long. About fifty cars go two hundred laps around the 2.5-mile (4 km) track. Even though these heavy cars are going 200 miles (322 km) per hour around a big oval track, it is okay for them to have contact. That is a nice way of saying that they can try to push one another out of the way!

FORMULA ONE RACING

Francesco Bernoulli is a Formula One race car. Every Formula One car is built and designed by its own team. Their secret design can change whenever they think of something that might work better. Formula One teams have the biggest budgets in the world—between $300 and $400 million! That money goes a long way in building the best car.

Built Right, Inside and Out

Designing a Formula One car isn't easy. Hard work goes into making sure that the body, wings, and spoilers provide the very best possible balance between drag, traction, and speed. When drivers are racing through the course's twisty turns, they want their tires stuck to the road. As a result, Formula One cars are a little bit slower than Indy cars—but not by much. Their top speed is still about 225 miles (360 km) per hour!

The Circuit

Formula One racers like circuits and street courses with plenty of twists, turns, and hills. Many Formula One circuits are a mix of street and track. The roads are closed to local traffic. This gives room for race cars to zoom up and down hills, around sharp turns, down narrow **straightaways**, and even through tunnels!

Formula One cars on the Monte Carlo circuit in Monaco

The Monaco Grand Prix

The most famous Formula One race is the Monaco Grand Prix in Europe. It takes place entirely on Monaco's city streets. The course is very narrow. It is also extremely dangerous. It is difficult for a driver to pass another car. This is one race in which a driver's skill is more important than the power of the car.

Monaco Grand Prix circuit

INDYCAR AND DRAG RACING

Jackson Storm has been clocked at an impressive 214 miles (344 km) per hour. But he wouldn't be able to keep up with the record-breaking speed of an Indy car or a top fuel dragster. An Indy car can reach a speed of 240 miles (385 km) per hour. A top fuel dragster goes almost 100 miles (160 km) per hour faster—that's an amazing 335 miles (540 km) per hour!

Indy Cars

All cars used in IndyCar racing have the exact same design. One company provides the chassis, and another provides the engine. Each car has the same body and parts. The difference lies in the driver. Because every car is the same, drivers depend on their skills at top speed on straightaways.

Most Indy cars race only in North America. Their most famous race is on the oval track of the **Indianapolis 500** in Indianapolis, Indiana.

Indianapolis 500

The Indianapolis 500 is a race held once a year at the Indianapolis Motor Speedway. It is just for Indy cars. The speedway is one of the biggest racetracks in the world. It has a giant 2.5 mile (4 km) oval track and a curvy track, too. Drivers make two hundred laps around the oval track. That's 500 miles (805 km) of racing!

The front straightaway at the 2015 Indianapolis 500

Drag Racing

The big lights turn green. Two cars race down a straight track for a quarter mile (0.4 km) as fast as they can! A drag race can feature all kinds of vehicles—even trucks and motorcycles. For a sports car, the whole race lasts less than fifteen seconds. If you race a top fuel dragster, you will finish by the time you count to four. It goes so fast that cars need parachutes to help them stop!

DEMOLITION DERBY, ENDURANCE, AND RALLY RACING

Raoul ÇaRoule is known as the World's Greatest Rally Car. He drives on any road surface and in all types of weather. Let's take a look at some races and events where skill, speed, and endurance are put to the test.

24 Hours of Le Mans Endurance Race

The **24 Hours of Le Mans** is an **endurance race** that lets drivers test how well cars hold up after twenty-four hours of high-speed driving. The race takes place on a nearly 8.5-mile (14 km) circuit that includes both a curvy track and closed streets. Pit stops in this race are as important as the driving. Tires are changed, and fuel tanks are filled. Sometimes repairs are made. Drivers jump out and make way for their driving partners. It is very exciting to watch!

A pit stop during the 24 Hours of Le Mans in 2014

World Rally Championship

Rally races take the driving off the paved road and onto ice, snow, gravel, and dirt. The **World Rally Championship (WRC)** is made up of thirteen three-day rallies that take place throughout the year. Each rally is held in a different country and is divided into fifteen to twenty-five stages. These stages can each be up to 15 miles (24 km) long. A driver and a codriver have to complete each stage in as little time as possible. World Rally cars look a lot like cars you see on the road. But they are lighter, more powerful, and just a bit safer.

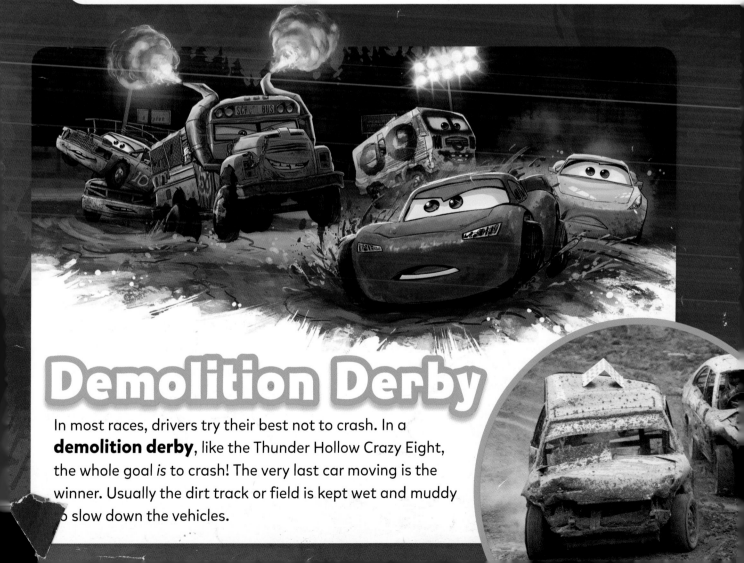

Demolition Derby

In most races, drivers try their best not to crash. In a **demolition derby**, like the Thunder Hollow Crazy Eight, the whole goal *is* to crash! The very last car moving is the winner. Usually the dirt track or field is kept wet and muddy to slow down the vehicles.

CARS OF THE FUTURE

Automobiles have changed quite a bit over the years—from a great legend like the Fabulous Hudson Hornet to a next-gen racer like Chase Racelott. Let's take a look at what the future might hold for everyday cars that cruise the roads.

Safer Cars

Making cars safer is an ongoing mission. Some cars now have cameras that show what's behind them. And some cars have special sensors to warn you about cars next to you. These sensors can tell if you are too close to another car. Some cars can even correct your steering or put on the brakes to avoid a crash.

Many new cars have airbags in the doors to protect you from a side-impact collision. Some carmakers are experimenting with airbags placed underneath a car to help stop a vehicle before a crash.

Driverless Cars

Would you ride in a car without a driver? Well, very soon you may have your chance! Many carmakers are testing driverless cars right now. These cars have cameras, lasers, radar, and special sensors to show them where to steer. These cars will be able to "talk" to one another so they stay out of one another's way. Soon you might be able to order a car without a driver to pick you up and take you to your destination.

Flying Cars?

Wouldn't it be fun to have a car that could lift itself into the air and fly to where you needed to go? Inventors have been imagining ways to do that for a long time.

There are a few flying cars today. But they look more like airplanes than cars. Most have long wings that unfold, and they need a runway to take off and land. The very best kind of flying car in the future might be one that can hop straight up into the air from the road. Some might have **rotors** like a helicopter's that unfold from the top. Others may use giant fans on the bottom of the car that push it into the air.

HIT THE ROAD!

We've learned so much about cars! We've learned that an automobile is made of many systems that work together—much like the racing team of Lightning and Cruz. We've learned how cars are made and about the impact a vehicle's design has on its performance and safety. And we've learned about lots of different race cars, types of races, and what we can expect in the not-too-distant future. So rev up your engines! It's going to be an exciting ride!

GLOSSARY

aerodynamic: designed in such a way so as to move through the air in a smooth and fast way

airbag: a device in a car designed to cushion a driver and passengers when activated in an accident

all-wheel drive (AWD): a drive system that uses sensors to automatically shift the power between the wheels as needed to get the best traction

aluminum: a strong and light silver metal commonly used in automobiles

antilock braking system: a system in some modern vehicles that prevents skidding and improves control by sensing and adjusting braking characteristics in individual wheels

assembly line: a manufacturing method in which parts are added as the car moves from workstation to workstation until it is finished

automatic transmission: a transmission system that automatically selects the best gear while driving

axle: a pin or metal shaft around which two wheels rotate

body: the outside shell of a car

brake pad: a thin block of friction-producing material attached to a caliper that squeezes against both sides of a brake disc when the brakes are applied

brake shoe: a curved steel plate covered with a thin block of friction-producing material that pushes against the inside of a brake drum when the brakes are applied

burnout: the deliberate spinning of the rear tires just before a drag race to heat the tires so they will stick to the track

caliper: the part of a disc brake that straddles both sides of the disc and clamps down on it when the brakes are applied

camshaft: a steel rod that controls the valves of an engine to open and close at the right time

carbon fiber: a strong, lightweight material that can replace many of the steel and aluminum parts of a car

ceramic: a strong, hard material often used to replace steel in many engine parts

chassis: the frame of a vehicle, onto which the engine, axles, and wheels are mounted

closed-wheel car: a kind of car where the body and trim of the car go over and around the wheels and tires

clutch pedal: a pedal that when engaged by a driver separates the engine from the transmission before changing gears

combustion: a controlled burning or explosion

composite: something that is created by mixing separate materials

compression: the process of pressing or squeezing things into a small space

crankshaft: a long metal rod in an engine that converts the up-and-down motion of the pistons into a rotating motion that sends power to the driving wheels

crash test dummy: a life-size model of a person used in crash tests to see what happens to the human body when a car gets into an accident

crumple zone: an area on a car that is designed to absorb most of the force in an accident

cylinder: the tube-shaped part of an engine block in which the pistons move up and down

Daytona 500: a 500-mile (805 km) NASCAR race that takes place yearly at Daytona International Speedway in Daytona Beach, Florida

demolition derby: a sport in which drivers deliberately crash into one another until only one car is left moving

disc brakes: the braking system on most modern cars that uses a brake pad attached to a caliper that squeezes both sides of a flat disc when the brakes are applied

disconnect: to break a connection

distributor: a device in the ignition system that sends electricity to each spark plug at just the right time to ignite the air and fuel mixture in the cylinders

downforce: a downward force produced by airflow around the body of a car

drag: the force from the air that slows a moving car

drag race: a short quarter-mile (0.4 km) race between two vehicles

drive system: a system that transfers the power from an engine to the wheels

drivetrain: the mechanical system that takes the rotating power from the engine and sends it out to the driving wheels of a motorized vehicle

drum brakes: the braking system on most older cars that uses brake shoes to push against the inside of the wheel drum when the brakes are applied

efficiency: doing or producing something without wasting energy, time, or materials

endurance race: a very long race that tests the ability of a car to drive over a long period of time

engine: a machine that uses the energy from a fuel such as gas to produce movement

epoxy: a kind of adhesive that when combined with carbon fibers makes a very strong and hard surface

exhaust: burned fuel created during the combustion process

exhaust system: the system that carries the burned fuel from the engine and out the tailpipe

exhaust valve: a valve that opens to let out the burned fuel

expand: to get bigger in size or force

Formula One race car: a single-seat, open-wheel race car that is specially designed by each race team. Formula One race cars are known as the fastest road course cars in the world.

four-wheel drive (4WD): a drive system that sends engine power to all four wheels at the same time

friction: the resistance to movement between two objects as they slide against each other

front-wheel drive (FWD): a drive system that sends the energy from the motor to just the front wheels

fuel: anything that can be used to create power

gear: a strong wheel with notches, or "teeth," that meshes with other gears to control the power from the engine to the wheels

ignite: to set or catch fire; to burn

Indianapolis 500: an annual 500-mile (805 km), two-hundred-lap IndyCar race held at the Indianapolis Motor Speedway in Indianapolis, Indiana

Indy car: a single-seat, open-wheel race car used in IndyCar racing. The chassis is built by only one company, and teams have a choice of only two approved engines.

intake: the step (or stroke) when the piston slides to the bottom of the cylinder and the intake valve opens to let in air and fuel

intake valve: a valve that opens to allow the fuel-air mixture into the cylinder and closes during the compression and combustion strokes

internal combustion: a process in which the fuel-air mixture inside an engine explodes to create a force that sends power to a drive system to move the wheels

manual transmission: a transmission system where the driver changes gear using the clutch and gear selector

motor: a device that converts any form of energy into mechanical energy to produce motion

motorized vehicle: any machine with wheels that gets the power to move from a motor or engine

NASCAR: the National Association for Stock Car Auto Racing, a US organization that governs and controls the sport of stock-car racing

open-wheel car: a kind of car where the wheels extend outside the body of the car

piston: a circular piece of metal that moves up and down inside a cylinder

pit stop: a quick stop for fuel, tires, and repairs during a car race

race car: a car designed to be fast that is driven in professional racing events

rally circuit: the course upon which a rally race is held

rear-wheel drive (RWD): a drive system that sends the energy from the motor to power just the rear wheels

rotor: a thin wing or a blade that produces a downdraft of air to move a helicopter upward

sensor: a device that finds and reacts to changes in things like heat, light, or movement

shock absorber: a combination of springs and a fluid- or air-filled tube that is connected to each wheel of a vehicle to reduce the force of sudden bumps or uneven surfaces on a road

spark plug: a device that supplies the electric spark to ignite the compressed air and fuel mixture at the top of the cylinder and make an explosion (combustion)

spoiler: an air deflector that is sometimes placed under the front bumper or on the rear end of a car to help keep it stable when traveling at high speeds

stock car: a race car that resembles a production car but is stronger and faster so it can be driven in special races

straightaway: the straight part of a road or race course where a driver may be able to pick up speed or pass another car

stroke: the distance traveled by a piston from its highest to lowest point in a cylinder. Stroke also refers to any of the four steps in the piston's operation: intake, compression, combustion, and exhaust.

traction: how well a car's spinning tires are able to grip the road or track without slipping

transfer: to move or change from one form or place to another

transmission: the part of a vehicle that uses various gears to transfer the power from the engine to the wheels

tread: the grooves on a tire that help it grip the road

tuner: a car that has been changed, or modified, to increase performance

24 Hours of Le Mans: an annual twenty-four-hour endurance race held in Le Mans, France

undercoating: a special kind of paint used on the bottom of a car that helps protect the frame from dirt and water

unibody: a method of automobile construction in which the chassis and body are made as one structure

wing: an aerodynamic device attached over the back of a car to cause a downward force and thus increase traction

World Rally Championship (WRC): an international race consisting of thirteen three-day events, or rallies, where teams race in timed stages. Each rally is held in a different country.

INDEX

PHOTO CREDITS

All photos are listed by page number from top to bottom.